The 7 Dimensions of Leadership

Empowering Leaders to Make the Ultimate Impact

The 7 Dimensions of Leadership

Empowering Leaders to Make the Ultimate Impact

Dr. Clinton P. Cornelius

Destiny & Victory Publishing

The 7 Dimensions of Leadership

ISBN: 978-1-962008-22-8

Printed in the United States of America

Published by Destiny & Victory Publishing

Table of Contents

Dedication 1

Introduction 3

Chapter 1: A True Servant Leader 7

Chapter 2: The Focused Leader 15

Chapter3: The Trained Leader 23

Chapter 4: Midnight Leader... 33

Chapter 5: Leading Beyond the Now 39

Chapter 6: A Well Leader 45

Chapter 7: The Leader of Leaders................................. 51

Conclusion.. 57

About The Author 61

Dedication

Dedicated to the legacy of my beloved mother, Mildred T. Cornelius Lewis, whose leadership was rooted in love, strength, and unwavering faith.

You led by example, teaching me that true leadership is not about position, but about serving others with humility and grace.

With all my love and gratitude,

your son & pastor,

Bubba

Introduction

Welcome to **The 7 Dimensions of Leadership: Empowering Leaders to Make the Ultimate Impact**. This book invites you to embark on a journey of discovering what it truly means to lead with purpose, influence, and integrity. It is about embracing leadership that extends beyond titles or positions, moving towards a kind of leadership that leaves a lasting impact on those we lead and the world around us.

In this book, we will explore the seven key dimensions that make up impactful leadership. These dimensions reflect the essential aspects of what it means to lead effectively in any sphere—whether it's within the church, business, community, or even within the family. Leadership, at its highest level, involves expanding your capacity to influence, inspire, and guide others toward a greater purpose.

Each of the seven dimensions is a vital building block in developing your leadership. They are not mere theories or abstract concepts but lived realities, modeled by the greatest leader of all time—Jesus Christ. His life provides timeless principles of leadership that have shaped history and continue to transform lives. His example teaches us how to lead with courage, vision, compassion, and strength. Through His leadership, we learn that true leadership requires constant growth and the willingness to serve and sacrifice for the greater good.

Why These Seven Dimensions?

The seven dimensions of leadership serve as a framework for helping leaders expand their effectiveness and make a significant impact. Each dimension explores a different aspect of leadership, offering both insights and practical tools that will enable you to grow as a leader. From becoming a servant leader to developing focus and perseverance, these dimensions are designed to help you rise to your full potential.

The path to effective leadership is filled with challenges, but those challenges serve to sharpen and refine us. They help us strengthen our resolve, clarify our vision, and increase our ability to influence. Leadership is dynamic—it is a journey of continuous learning and adaptation. As we grow in each of these seven dimensions, we are better equipped to face the trials that come with leadership, making us stronger and more effective in our roles.

Preparing to Make the Ultimate Impact

As you read through the chapters in this book, take time to reflect on your own leadership journey. Consider how you can apply these principles in your life, your ministry, or your organization. Think about the leaders who have influenced and inspired you and how you can, in turn, influence the next generation of leaders.

I encourage you to approach this book with a heart and mind open to new insights and challenges. The seven dimensions of leadership will not only help you grow but will empower you to make the ultimate impact in every area of your life.

Welcome to **The 7 Dimensions of Leadership**. Let's begin the journey of growth, empowerment, and lasting impact.

The 7 Dimensions of Leadership

Chapter 1
A True Servant Leader

What does it mean to be a true servant leader? A servant leader is one who chooses the *towel* over the *title*. He recognizes that leadership is not about position or accolades but about serving others. Jesus Himself exemplified this in John 13:4-5 (KJV), where the Word of God tells us, *"He riseth from supper, and laid aside his garments; and took a towel, and girded himself. After that he poureth water into a bason, and began to wash the disciples' feet, and to wipe them with the towel wherewith he was girded."* Jesus, the greatest of all, took on the role of a servant, washing the feet of His disciples, teaching us that the greatest among us must be willing to serve.

A servant leader, therefore, is one who puts others before themselves. They select the towel, willing to do the hard work, to go the extra mile, and to make personal sacrifices. It's not about people serving the leader, but about the leader serving others. Matthew 20:26-27 (KJV) confirms this principle: *"But it shall not be so among you: but whosoever will be great among you, let him be your minister; And whosoever will be chief among you, let him be your servant."* The servant leader knows that true greatness comes from serving others.

Going the Extra Mile

A servant leader is not satisfied with doing just the minimum; they always go the extra mile. Jesus taught this in Matthew 5:41 (KJV), *"And whosoever shall compel thee to go a mile, go with him twain."* This principle teaches that a servant leader doesn't just fulfill the basic obligations but goes above and beyond to serve and uplift others. Servant leadership is about sacrificing for the greater good—sacrificing time, energy, and resources to benefit others.

The cost of leadership is often high. It demands time and sacrifice. As a servant leader, you will find that leadership requires you to sacrifice your personal time, your talents, and even your desires. Sometimes, it means taking a back seat, allowing others to shine while you serve quietly in the background. Philippians 2:3 (KJV) encourages this mindset: *"Let nothing be done through strife or vainglory; but in lowliness of mind let each esteem other better than themselves."* Servant leadership is about putting others first and sacrificing for their benefit.

Misconceptions About Servant Leadership

There are many misconceptions about servant leadership. One common misconception is that being a servant leader makes you a slave. However, this is far from the truth. A slave is forced to serve, while a servant leader chooses to serve willingly. Galatians 5:13 (KJV) says, *"For, brethren, ye have been called unto liberty; only use not liberty for an occasion to the flesh, but by love serve one another."* We serve not out of obligation but out of love and commitment to others.

Another misconception is that servant leadership entitles you to certain privileges. Some may think that because they are a leader, they deserve respect and recognition without earning it. However, true servant leadership is about earning respect through humility and service, not through entitlement. Luke 22:26 (KJV) reinforces this: *"But ye shall not be so: but he that is greatest among you, let him be as the younger; and he that is chief, as he that doth serve."* Servant leaders are not entitled to privileges; they lead by example, through service and humility.

Personal Reflections on Servant Leadership

In my own journey as a servant leader, I have had to confront misconceptions that I once held. I used to think that being a servant leader meant always stepping back and allowing others to take the lead. However, I've learned that there are times when servant leadership requires stepping forward. There are doors of opportunity that God opens, and it is our responsibility as leaders to walk through them. Just because we are servants does not mean we should avoid the opportunities God places before us.

One example of this can be found in my own life. There were times when I was in rooms filled with other leaders, and I mistakenly thought that my role as a servant leader meant I should remain silent. However, I realized that there are moments when God places us in those rooms to speak up, to lead, and to contribute. Servant leadership does not mean shying away from responsibility—it means stepping into the roles God has called us to while maintaining a heart of service.

Biblical Examples of Servant Leaders

There are many examples of servant leaders in the Bible. One such example is Nehemiah. Nehemiah was a cupbearer to the king, a servant by profession. Yet, when God placed a burden on his heart to rebuild the walls of Jerusalem, he stepped into the role of leadership. Nehemiah 2:5 (KJV) says, *"And I said unto the king, If it please the king, and if thy servant have found favour in thy sight, that thou wouldest send me unto Judah, unto the city of my fathers' sepulchres, that I may build it."* Nehemiah led the people with a servant's heart, but he also displayed great courage, strategy, and determination in fulfilling his God-given assignment.

Joshua is another example of a servant leader. He served under Moses for many years before stepping into the role of leadership. Joshua 1:2 (KJV) tells us, *"Moses my servant is dead; now therefore arise, go over this Jordan, thou, and all this people, unto the land which I do give to them, even to the children of Israel."* Joshua served faithfully, and when it was his time, God elevated him to lead the people into the Promised Land.

David also exemplifies servant leadership. He served his father by tending sheep and later served King Saul. Even after being anointed as king, David continued to serve humbly until the appointed time for him to take the throne. David's heart for service is evident in his actions, from caring for his father's sheep to leading the men in the cave of Adullam. 1 Samuel 22:2 (KJV) describes David's leadership: *"And every one that was in distress, and every one that was in debt, and every one that was discontented, gathered themselves unto him; and he became a captain over them."* David's servant leadership transformed these men into mighty warriors.

Lessons from Nehemiah and David

There are powerful lessons we can learn from the lives of Nehemiah and David. From Nehemiah, we learn the importance of staying focused on the task at hand. When others tried to distract him from rebuilding the wall, Nehemiah's response was clear: *"I am doing a great work, so that I cannot come down" (Nehemiah 6:3, KJV).* As servant leaders, we must stay committed to the work God has given us, despite opposition or distractions.

From David, we learn the importance of taking care of the small details. Before David ever faced Goliath, he made sure that someone was watching over his father's sheep. 1 Samuel 17:20 (KJV) says, *"And David rose up early in the morning, and left the sheep with a keeper, and took, and went, as Jesse had commanded him."* David's attention to the small things prepared him for the larger tasks that lay ahead.

Misconceptions and Mistakes of Servant Leaders

Servant leaders must be cautious of common mistakes. One mistake is falling in love with the title rather than the task. As leaders, we must remember that the position we hold is not about elevating ourselves but about serving others. Another mistake is not knowing when to let go. Ecclesiastes 3:1 (KJV) reminds us, *"To every thing there is a season, and a time to every purpose under the heaven."* There comes a time when we must let go of one season and embrace the next, trusting God's timing.

It is also important to avoid comparing yourself to others. Each leader has their own unique assignment, and comparing yourself to others can lead to discontentment and distraction from your purpose. 2 Corinthians 10:12 (KJV) says, *"For we dare not make ourselves of the number, or compare ourselves with some that commend themselves:*

but they measuring themselves by themselves, and comparing themselves among themselves, are not wise." Instead of comparing, focus on fulfilling your God-given purpose and calling, recognizing that God's assignments are unique to each individual.

Additionally, don't become married to a position. Positions are temporary, but our calling to serve remains. When the season changes, be willing to move on to what God has next.

Reasons to Be a Servant Leader

Why would someone choose to be a servant leader? Here are a few reasons:

1. **Giving to Others Brings Blessings:** One of the main reasons I want to be a servant leader is because as I give to others and bless them, the Lord, in turn, blesses me. Luke 6:38 (KJV) says, *"Give, and it shall be given unto you; good measure, pressed down, and shaken together, and running over, shall men give into your bosom."* The principle of sowing and reaping is clear: when I sow into others' lives, God blesses my own life abundantly.

2. **Following the Attitude of Christ:** I want to be a servant leader because it reflects the attitude of Christ. Jesus said in

Matthew 23:11, KJV , *"But he that is greatest among you shall be your servant."* Serving others aligns with Christ's example, and there is no greater honor than following His model of leadership.

3. **The Satisfaction of Seeing Others Grow:** There is a deep satisfaction in witnessing someone else improve because of my influence. Serving others and helping them reach their potential brings me joy, and I believe that as I assist others in achieving

their dreams, God will also fulfill my own aspirations. Philippians 2:4 (KJV) reminds us to focus on others' needs, which brings me joy, knowing that God will honor my efforts and fulfill His promises in my life.

4. **Influencing and Impacting Lives:** My desire to be a servant leader stems from the positive impact I can make on others. Proverbs 11:25 (KJV) highlights that when we bless others generously, we are also blessed in return. Pouring into others' lives enriches both them and ourselves. There is no greater reward than seeing others flourish through the influence we have on their lives.

5. **Solving Problems That Bother You:** Like Nehemiah, servant leaders are often motivated by problems that bother them deeply. Nehemiah was driven to rebuild the wall of Jerusalem because the brokenness of the city distressed him. Nehemiah 2:17 (KJV) says, *"Then said I unto them, Ye see the distress that we are in, how Jerusalem lieth waste, and the gates thereof are burned with fire: come, and let us build up the wall of Jerusalem, that we be no more a reproach."* Being a servant leader allows you to address the circumstances and situations that burden your heart, offering a solution through your service.

Conclusion

A true servant leader embodies the heart of Christ, choosing the towel over the title, and placing others' needs before their own. Through humility, sacrifice, and an unwavering commitment to serve, the servant leader transforms not only individuals but entire communities. Like Nehemiah and David, servant leaders stay focused on their God-given assignments, attend to the small details, and persevere despite challenges. They find joy in lifting others, seeing lives transformed through their influence, and solving problems that align with God's purposes. Ultimately, a servant leader's legacy is not defined by position but by the lasting impact made through selfless service.

Marinate for an Impact:

1. How does the example of Jesus washing His disciples' feet challenge your understanding of leadership and service?

2. In what ways can you go the extra mile in your current roles, demonstrating servant leadership through sacrifice?

3. Reflect on a time when you were called to step forward as a leader. How did you balance stepping into the role while maintaining a heart of service?

Chapter 2
The Focused Leader

A focused leader is one who centers their attention, thoughts, and actions on God's Word. When we talk about focus in a biblical sense, we are discussing directing our attention toward God's Word, which encompasses His principles, His will, and His ways. God's Word helps us align our lives according to His purpose, enabling us to fulfill the role He has called us to without being distracted by other things. This is the essence of focus.

Defining a Focused Leader

With that definition in mind, what does it mean to be a focused leader? A focused leader is someone who is:

1. **Faithful to the Task:** They understand their calling and remain committed to it. Luke 16:10 (KJV) says, *"He that is faithful in that which is least is faithful also in much: and he that is unjust in the*

least is unjust also in much." A focused leader remains faithful no matter the task they are assigned.

2. **Oversees Responsibility:** A focused leader recognizes that they have been appointed to a particular task and diligently oversees the things they have been entrusted with. Colossians 3:23 (KJV) says, *"And whatsoever ye do, do it heartily, as to the Lord, and not unto men."* The focused leader carries out their responsibility with excellence.

3. **Continues to Learn and Grow:** A focused leader does not become complacent but commits to continuous learning and growth. Psalm 78:72 (KJV) says, *"So he fed them according to the integrity of his heart; and guided them by the skilfulness of his hands."* This reminds us that leaders must feed others from their heart as they grow in wisdom and grace.

Managing Versus Leading

A focused leader understands the difference between managing and leading. Managing often involves maintaining the status quo, but leading requires guiding people toward growth and progress. It's possible to hold a title and simply manage, but leading requires going beyond maintaining and stepping into serving others.

A focused leader also understands the difference between a *towel* and a *title*. The towel represents service. A leader who takes up the towel is willing to serve others, even if it means doing the hard, humble work. The title represents the position, but the towel represents the heart of leadership. John 13:14 (KJV) shows us the importance of this: *"If I then, your Lord and Master, have washed your feet; ye also ought to wash one another's feet."* Jesus modeled servant leadership by taking up the towel and washing His disciples' feet.

Setting Excellent Examples

A focused leader sets excellent examples for others to follow. 1 Timothy 4:12 (KJV) encourages us, *"Let no man despise thy youth; but be thou an example of the believers, in word, in conversation, in charity, in spirit, in faith, in purity."* By setting a standard of excellence, a focused leader creates a culture of growth and integrity within their organization, ministry, or household.

This kind of leadership influences others to adopt these values. A focused leader not only leads with excellence but also creates a pathway for others to follow. Whether it's within a church, a school board, or any organization, leading with excellence paves the way for others to succeed.

Leading Well

A focused leader also leads well, recognizing that they are not alone in their leadership. Proverbs 11:14 (KJV) says, *"Where no counsel is, the people fall: but in the multitude of counsellors there is safety."* Leading well means involving others, seeking counsel, and utilizing the strengths of the team. Leaders need followers, and a focused leader knows how to engage others in their responsibility, helping them reach their full potential.

Making Adjustments and Eliminating Background Noise

A focused leader is also one who constantly makes adjustments. Just as athletes adjust their techniques to improve their performance, a focused leader must adapt to the changing dynamics of their environment. Philippians 3:13 (KJV) says, *"Brethren, I count not myself to have apprehended: but this one thing I do, forgetting those things which are behind, and reaching forth unto those things which are before."* To remain focused, a leader must eliminate background noise, which includes distractions from the past or present that try to pull them off course.

Background noise can include criticism, negative opinions, or even memories of past failures. Isaiah 43:18-19 (KJV) reminds us, *"Remember ye not the former things, neither consider the things of old. Behold, I will do a new thing; now it shall spring forth; shall ye not know it?"* A focused leader must stay forward-looking, trusting in God's new direction.

Heeding the Voice of Influence

A focused leader listens to the voices of influence in their life, including mentors, pastors, and especially the Holy Spirit. Proverbs 19:20 (KJV) says, *"Hear counsel, and receive instruction, that thou mayest be wise in thy latter end."* Listening to trusted voices allows leaders to remain focused and aligned with God's will. The Holy Spirit is our ultimate guide in leadership, as He directs our steps and gives wisdom in difficult situations.

Avoiding Distractions and Disconnection

One of the key challenges a focused leader faces is avoiding distractions. Distractions can come in many forms—personal issues, opinions from others, or unnecessary activities. Hebrews 12:1 (KJV) reminds us to *"lay aside every weight, and the sin which doth so easily beset us,"* and to stay focused on our God-given race.

Another danger is disconnection. When a leader becomes disconnected, like a coffee pot that isn't plugged in, they lose their effectiveness. John 15:4 (KJV) says, *"Abide in me, and I in you. As the branch cannot bear fruit of itself, except it abide in the vine; no more can ye, except ye abide in me."* Staying connected to God, and to the people you lead, ensures that you remain fruitful and effective in your leadership.

The Unfocused Leader: Saul

Not every leader remains focused. A prime example of an unfocused leader is King Saul. Saul started well but lost his focus by listening to the opinions of the people rather than following the direct command of God. In 1 Samuel 15:13-14 (KJV), the prophet Samuel confronted Saul, saying, *"And Samuel came to Saul: and Saul said unto him, Blessed be thou of the Lord: I have performed the commandment of the Lord. And Samuel said, What meaneth then this bleating of the sheep in mine ears, and the lowing of the oxen which I hear?"* Saul had disobeyed God by sparing the best of the livestock after being instructed to destroy everything.

Samuel then reminded Saul in 1 Samuel 15:22 (KJV), *"Behold, to obey is better than sacrifice, and to hearken than the fat of rams."* Saul's failure to remain focused on God's specific instructions led to his downfall. Instead of being focused on his assignment, Saul was influenced by the people and their desires. This loss of focus caused him to lose the kingdom. The lesson we learn from Saul is the importance of remaining steadfast in the task God has commanded us to do, without being swayed by the opinions of others.

Biblical Examples of Focused Leaders

Several leaders in the Bible exemplify focused leadership:

1. **Nehemiah** remained focused as he rebuilt the walls of Jerusalem. Despite opposition and distractions, Nehemiah refused to come down from the wall. Nehemiah 6:3 (KJV) says, *"And I sent messengers unto them, saying, I am doing a great*

work, so that I cannot come down." Nehemiah's focus allowed him to complete the work God had called him to do.

2. **Moses** stayed focused even when facing immense pressure. When the people of Israel complained, Moses continually sought God for help, remaining steadfast in his leadership. Exodus 14:15-16 (KJV) says, *"And the Lord said unto Moses, Wherefore criest thou unto me? speak unto the children of Israel, that they go forward."* Moses understood the importance of using what was in his hand and leading the people forward.

3. **Paul** also demonstrates focused leadership. He writes in Philippians 3:14 (KJV), *"I press toward the mark for the prize of the high calling of God in Christ Jesus."* Paul was focused on his mission despite persecution and suffering, keeping his eyes on the ultimate goal.

Staying Focused

In conclusion, to be a focused leader means to remain committed to the task God has given you, continually grow and learn, avoid distractions, and stay connected to the source of your strength—God. Remember to listen to the voices of influence in your life and seek wisdom from God and trusted mentors. Stay faithful to the responsibilities entrusted to you and lead others with excellence, setting an example that others can follow.

Remember, just as Nehemiah stayed focused on the wall, and Moses used what was in his hand, you too can remain focused and fulfill the calling God has placed on your life. Avoid the pitfalls of leaders like Saul, who lost focus by allowing the opinions of others to override God's clear commands. Let your focus remain on God's purpose and His will, and you will succeed in your leadership journey.

Conclusion

A focused leader is one who remains steadfast in their calling, continually seeking God's direction and staying connected to His Word. By faithfully overseeing their responsibilities, avoiding distractions, and staying connected to trusted voices, such leaders set a powerful example for others to follow. Nehemiah, Moses, and Paul exemplified what it means to be focused leaders, maintaining their course despite opposition and challenges. As you lead, remain committed to God's purpose, stay focused on the task at hand, and allow His wisdom to guide your steps. In doing so, you will fulfill the calling placed on your life and lead others toward their God-given destinies.

Marinate for an Impact:

1. How can you ensure that your focus remains centered on God's Word and purpose, even when distractions arise?

2. In what areas of your leadership do you need to adjust or eliminate background noise to maintain your focus and effectiveness?

3. Reflecting on biblical examples like Nehemiah and Paul, what steps can you take to remain steadfast in the tasks God has assigned to you?

The 7 Dimensions of Leadership

Chapter 3
The Trained Leader

B efore we delve into what it means to be a trained leader, it's important to understand the dangers of being a toxic leader.

Training and mentorship are cornerstones of leadership development within the body of Christ. Just as Paul mentored Timothy, leaders today are called to raise up others to fulfill their God-given potential. However, while mentorship is crucial, it is essential to recognize the potential for toxicity within these relationships. Toxic leadership and mentorship can cause great harm, stifling growth and wounding those who are meant to be nurtured and trained.

Understanding Toxicity in Leadership

Toxic leadership is more than imperfection or inexperience. It refers to behavior that is harmful and detrimental to those under a leader's care. Scripture teaches us that a small amount of something harmful can corrupt the whole body: *"A little leaven leaveneth the whole lump"*

(Galatians 5:9, KJV). In the same way, toxic leadership can spread throughout a ministry, causing damage far beyond the immediate relationship. Toxic behavior includes the abuse of authority, manipulation, and control—actions that damage both the mentee and the broader community.

It is important to distinguish between imperfection and toxicity. Not every mistake or weakness in leadership constitutes toxicity. Some leaders are simply inexperienced or lack training, but that does not make them toxic. Toxicity arises when authority is consistently abused, and when control is exerted over others in a way that damages their spiritual, emotional, or physical well-being.

The Abuse of Authority

Abuse of authority is one of the clearest indicators of toxic leadership. God has given leaders authority to guide His people, but that authority must be exercised with love, humility, and care. Jesus warned His disciples against the misuse of power: *"Ye know that the princes of the Gentiles exercise dominion over them... But it shall not be so among you"* (Matthew 20:25-26, KJV). When a leader begins to control, manipulate, or harm others through their authority, they have crossed into toxicity.

There is a difference between godly correction and toxic behavior. Correction is a necessary part of leadership, as Proverbs 3:12 (KJV) reminds us: *"For whom the Lord loveth he correcteth; even as a father the son in whom he delighteth."* However, when correction is used as a tool for humiliation, manipulation, or control, it becomes harmful. Leaders must be vigilant to ensure that their correction builds up rather than tears down.

Cloning vs. Cultivating: The Dangers of Imitation

Toxic leadership can also manifest through the attempt to clone mentees. A toxic mentor may try to mold their mentees into replicas of themselves, demanding that they adopt the same personality, style, or methods. This denies the unique gifts and callings that God has placed within each individual. *"For as we have many members in one body, and all members have not the same office"* (Romans 12:4, KJV). A healthy mentor cultivates the individuality of their mentees, helping them grow in their unique calling rather than forcing them into a specific mold.

When a leader attempts to clone a mentee, they stifle that person's development, causing them to feel inadequate or unworthy. This type of leadership breeds insecurity and frustration, as the mentee struggles to fit into a role that was never meant for them. In contrast, a godly mentor recognizes the diversity of gifts within the body of Christ and encourages their mentees to grow into the leaders God has called them to be.

The Role of Compassion in Leadership

Another hallmark of toxic leadership is a lack of compassion. Jesus modeled compassion throughout His ministry, and He calls us to do the same: *"Be ye therefore merciful, as your Father also is merciful"* (Luke 6:36, KJV). Compassionate leadership seeks to uplift and support others, offering grace and mercy in times of need. Toxic leaders, however, often use harsh methods to control or punish, creating an environment of fear and shame.

True leadership requires a balance of discipline and grace. While correction is necessary, it must be done in a way that reflects the love and mercy of God. Leaders who fail to show compassion are not reflecting the heart of Christ, and their leadership becomes a source of pain rather than growth. As leaders, we must remember that it is the kindness of God that leads to repentance (Romans 2:4, KJV), not fear or intimidation.

Stewardship vs. Ownership

One of the key issues that leads to toxic leadership is the failure to distinguish between stewardship and ownership. As leaders, we are called to be stewards of God's people, not their owners. *"The earth is the Lord's, and the fulness thereof; the world, and they that dwell therein"* (Psalm 24:1, KJV). Toxic leaders, however, often act as though the people they lead belong to them, exerting control over every aspect of their lives. This overreach leads to isolation, manipulation, and emotional harm.

A godly leader understands that their role is to guide and nurture, not to dominate. They respect the individuality of those under their care and encourage them to grow in their own God-given gifts and callings. Toxic leaders, on the other hand, may attempt to micromanage every detail of their mentees' lives, leading to an unhealthy dependence and a loss of personal freedom.

Recognizing and Addressing Toxicity

Recognizing toxic leadership is the first step in addressing it. Toxicity often manifests through control, manipulation, and the stifling of individuality. If a leader is constantly humiliating, isolating, or controlling those they lead, it is a sign of toxic behavior. In such cases, both the leader and the mentee must seek to correct these behaviors before they cause lasting damage.

Leaders must be willing to reflect on their own behavior and make adjustments when necessary. Likewise, mentees should not be afraid to address concerns or seek help when they find themselves in a toxic situation. Scripture teaches us the importance of seeking wisdom and counsel: *"Where no counsel is, the people fall: but in the multitude of counsellors there is safety"* (Proverbs 11:14, KJV). Sometimes, addressing toxic leadership may involve confronting the issue directly, while in other cases, it may require seeking outside support or even leaving the situation if it cannot be resolved.

From Toxicity to Training

Having explored the signs and dangers of toxic leadership, we now turn our attention to the qualities of a trained leader. A trained leader is the antithesis of a toxic leader. They are individuals who have been refined through the Word of God, equipped to lead with grace, wisdom, and humility.

The Trained Leader

The Word of God tells us in Genesis 14:14 (KJV), *"And when Abram heard that his brother was taken captive, he armed his trained servants, born in his own house, three hundred and eighteen, and pursued them unto Dan."* This scripture demonstrates the importance of being not just a leader, but a trained leader. Abraham's trained servants were prepared for the task ahead, and they were able to go out and help rescue his nephew Lot. This principle is essential for us today as leaders—we must not only be in a position of leadership but be trained and equipped for the challenges we will face.

Why Do We Need to Be Trained Leaders?

The need for training as a leader is critical. An untrained leader can easily get off track, making poor decisions and losing sight of their mission. Proverbs 19:2 (KJV) reminds us, *"Also, that the soul be without knowledge, it is not good; and he that hasteth with his feet sinneth."* A lack of training can lead to error and inefficiency. If a leader is untrained, they may not be able to effectively guide the people they are responsible for, leading to confusion and mismanagement.

One of the dangers of being an untrained leader is that you may not understand the needs and conditions of the people you are leading. Proverbs 27:23 (KJV) says, *"Be thou diligent to know the state of thy flocks, and look well to thy herds."* As a leader, you must know the state of your people—what they are going through, what they need, and how best to guide them. If you are not trained, you may unintentionally neglect the needs of those you lead, causing them to lose direction and confidence in your leadership.

The Characteristics of a Trained Leader

1. **Knows His People:** A trained leader knows the people he leads. This means understanding their strengths, weaknesses, and capacities. Just as Abraham knew his trained servants, a trained leader is familiar with the people in their care. 1 Peter 5:2 (KJV) advises, *"Feed the flock of God which is among you, taking the oversight thereof, not by constraint, but willingly; not for filthy lucre, but of a ready mind."* Knowing your people allows you to guide them effectively.

2. **Knows Himself:** A trained leader also knows himself. He is aware of his strengths, weaknesses, and limitations. This self-awareness is crucial because it allows the leader to work within their abilities and seek help in areas where they may fall short. 2 Corinthians 13:5 (KJV) says, *"Examine yourselves, whether ye be in the faith; prove your own selves."* A trained leader regularly reflects on their actions and attitudes to ensure they are in line with God's will.

3. **Understands Timing:** Timing is vital for a trained leader. Ecclesiastes 3:1 (KJV) reminds us, *"To every thing there is a season, and a time to every purpose under the heaven."* Understanding the importance of timing can determine whether a leader's actions will be successful or not. My former pastor, Pastor Pollard, often reminded me that you can do the right thing at the wrong time and miss the intended impact. Knowing when to act is just as important as knowing what to do.

4. **Applies Their Training:** It is not enough to receive training; a trained leader must apply what they have learned. James 1:22 (KJV) warns, *"But be ye doers of the word, and not hearers only, deceiving your own selves."* A trained leader takes the knowledge they have gained and puts it into practice. Hearing the training is one thing, but living it out is what makes a leader effective.

Being Open to Change

One of the mistakes that a trained leader must avoid is being closed off to change. Training is not just about learning facts; it's about developing the flexibility to adapt to new situations and challenges. Philippians 3:13 (KJV) says, *"Brethren, I count not myself to have apprehended: but this one thing I do, forgetting those things which are behind, and reaching forth unto those things which are before."* A trained leader remains open to change, recognizing that growth often requires adjustment and adaptation.

Flexibility is key to effective leadership. The more flexible you are, the better equipped you are to handle unexpected changes and challenges. A trained leader must be willing to adjust their approach as the situation demands, without compromising their core values and mission.

The Importance of Navigating, Negotiating, and Nurturing

A trained leader must also know how to navigate through difficult situations, negotiate when necessary, and nurture those who are hurting or in need of support. Ephesians 4:29 (KJV) encourages us, *"Let no corrupt communication proceed out of your mouth, but that which is good to the use of edifying, that it may minister grace unto the hearers."*

- **Navigating:** Navigating conflict and challenges is essential. A trained leader knows how to lead through difficult terrain, keeping their eyes on the goal while guiding their people safely through obstacles.

- **Negotiating:** Negotiation involves finding common ground and making decisions that benefit the group as a whole. Proverbs 15:22 (KJV) says, *"Without counsel purposes are disappointed: but in the multitude of counsellors they are established."* A trained leader knows when and how to negotiate to achieve the best outcome for all involved.

- **Nurturing:** Nurturing refers to caring for the needs of those under your leadership. A trained leader takes the time to minister to the emotional, spiritual, and sometimes physical needs of their people, helping them recover and thrive.

Avoiding Common Mistakes

A trained leader must also be careful to avoid some common pitfalls. One such mistake is assuming that simply hearing or knowing something automatically makes you an expert. True leadership comes from applying what you know. Another mistake is failing to be flexible or adaptable. A rigid leader will struggle to navigate changing circumstances and may miss opportunities for growth or improvement.

Another critical mistake is failing to understand timing. As mentioned earlier, doing the right thing at the wrong time can be just as detrimental as doing the wrong thing altogether. Patience and discernment are key qualities of a trained leader.

Conclusion: Becoming a Trained Leader

Becoming a trained leader requires dedication, self-awareness, and a commitment to applying what you have learned. Like Abraham's trained servants, we must be prepared and equipped for the tasks ahead. We must know the people we lead, know ourselves, and understand the importance of timing in every situation. We must remain open to change, flexible in our approach, and committed to navigating, negotiating, and nurturing the people God has entrusted to us.

A trained leader stands in stark contrast to a toxic leader. While toxic leadership manipulates and controls, the trained leader uplifts, cultivates, and leads with wisdom, grace, and a deep reliance on God. The trained leader understands the balance between godly correction and compassion, steering clear of the abuses of authority that lead to toxic environments.

Remember, a trained leader is not just someone who holds a position, but someone who leads with wisdom, understanding, and care. Let us commit ourselves to the process of training and growth so that we may lead effectively, to the glory of God.

Marinate for an Impact:

1. How has this chapter changed your understanding of the importance of being a trained leader?

2. How can you begin applying the principles of trained leadership in your current role?

3. Reflecting on the importance of timing, how can you better discern the right moment to act in your leadership decisions?

Chapter 4
Midnight Leader

As leaders, we often find ourselves in painful situations. It's in the midst of this pain that we must learn how to lead effectively, even when every step feels like a struggle. In Acts 16, we see the story of Paul and Silas as they found themselves in one of these painful situations. They were trying to do the right thing—doing the work of the Lord—but instead of being rewarded, they were beaten and imprisoned. This chapter focuses on what it means to be a *Midnight Leader*—a leader who knows how to lead through the pain.

The Pain of Leadership

Oftentimes, as a leader, pain arises from betrayal. Someone you lead, someone you've helped, may turn against you. This betrayal is painful, especially when you've invested so much into them. It can also be painful to feel unappreciated or misunderstood. You pour out your heart, you give your all, but it feels like it's never enough. These situations can weigh heavily on a leader's heart.

In Acts 16, Paul and Silas experienced this very thing. They were stripped and beaten for doing the work of God, and their pain led them to prison. As leaders, we must be careful not to let the pain we experience lock us up—whether it locks up our ability to continue, our desire to care, or our capacity to trust others. It's easy to find ourselves locking up our hearts and isolating ourselves because of the pain.

Psalm 41:9 (KJV) speaks to this kind of betrayal: *"Yea, mine own familiar friend, in whom I trusted, which did eat of my bread, hath lifted up his heel against me."* Betrayal can cause us to close off, but a midnight leader must learn how to push through the pain.

Locking Yourself Up

Pain has the ability to lock us up in more ways than one. As a leader, you might find yourself withdrawing from those around you, becoming distant because you've been hurt. You may not want to be upfront anymore or trust anyone because of the wounds you carry. Proverbs 18:1 (KJV) warns against isolation: *"Through desire a man, having separated himself, seeketh and intermeddleth with all wisdom."* Isolation can prevent us from being effective leaders.

For instance, as a senior pastor in the local church, you may find yourself trying to manage and control everything because you no longer trust others to carry the load with you. You say you're leading, but in reality, you're leading in isolation. You're doing everything yourself because you fear being hurt again. This is how pain imprisons us.

This kind of isolation doesn't only affect church leadership; it can also play out in nonprofits, board positions, or even at home. When you've been betrayed, it's easy to shut down and lock up. However, this only leads to burnout and frustration because you can't effectively influence others if you don't trust them. Proverbs 3:5 (KJV) reminds us, *"Trust in the Lord with all thine heart; and lean not unto thine own understanding."* As leaders, we must remember to place our trust in God, even when people fail us.

Recognizing the Pain but Pressing On

It's important to acknowledge the pain—don't sweep it under the rug or pretend it doesn't exist. Pain is real, but in the midst of it, we must press on. Pain is temporary, and eventually, it will change. Romans 8:18 (KJV) says, *"For I reckon that the sufferings of this present time are not worthy to be compared with the glory which shall be revealed in us."* Though the pain is great, the promise of what's to come is greater.

So, how do you lead through the pain? First, you must put things in order. Realize that the people who cause you pain are often hurting themselves. Hurt people hurt people. Recognize that pain is part of the human experience and that everyone, at some point, will cause or experience pain. This is the first step in leading through it.

Second, admit that the pain is there, but decide that you will get through your midnight. Midnight represents the darkest part of the night, but it's also a transition to a new day. Lamentations 3:22-23 (KJV) tells us, *"It is of the Lord's mercies that we are not consumed, because his compassions fail not. They are new every morning: great is thy faithfulness."* Even in the darkest moments, God's mercy is renewed every morning.

Praying Through the Pain

One of the most critical things you must do as a midnight leader is pray through the pain. When Paul and Silas were beaten and thrown into prison, they prayed. Acts 16:25 (KJV) says, *"And at midnight Paul and Silas prayed, and sang praises unto God: and the prisoners heard them."* Despite their circumstances, they turned to God in prayer and praise.

Prayer is vital because it keeps us connected to the source of our strength. It reminds us that we are not alone in our struggles. Philippians 4:6-7 (KJV) instructs us, *"Be careful for nothing; but in every thing by prayer and supplication with thanksgiving let your requests be made known unto God. And the peace of God, which passeth all understanding, shall keep your hearts and minds through Christ Jesus."* In times of pain, prayer brings peace.

The Power of Praise

After they prayed, Paul and Silas began to praise God, even though they were still in pain and still in prison. This act of praise unlocked something in the spiritual realm. Acts 16:26 (KJV) tells us, *"And suddenly there was a great earthquake, so that the foundations of the prison were shaken: and immediately all the doors were opened, and every one's bands were loosed."* Their praise brought about their deliverance.

As leaders, we must learn to praise God through the pain. Praise invites the presence and power of God into our situation. It shifts our focus from our circumstances to the God who is greater than our pain. Psalm 34:1 (KJV) says, *"I will bless the Lord at all times: his praise shall continually be in my mouth."* Praising God in the midst of pain invites His power to work in our lives.

Leading with the Power of God

The power of God is essential for every midnight leader. It's God's power that will push you through the pain and pull you out on the other side. As leaders, we cannot rely on our own strength; we must depend on God's power. Zechariah 4:6 (KJV) says, *"Not by might, nor by power, but by my spirit, saith the Lord of hosts."*

God's power gives us the courage to keep going, even when everything in us wants to quit. It gives us the wisdom to lead effectively, even in difficult times. It gives us the strength to persevere like a bulldog that refuses to let go. With the power of God, we can overcome betrayal, isolation, and pain. 2 Corinthians 12:9 (KJV) reminds us, *"My grace is sufficient for thee: for my strength is made perfect in weakness."* In our weakest moments, God's strength is made manifest.

Personal Testimony: Leading Through Midnight

I've faced many midnight seasons in my own life. I remember a time when I lost both my mother and grandmother within four months of each other. At the same time, I was leading my church through a major transition. It was one of the most painful seasons of my life. There were days when all I could do was cry, and other days when I wondered why I had to endure such heartache.

But through it all, I continued to lead. The people in my church saw me cry, they saw my pain, but they also saw me lean on God for strength. In my midnight hour, I had to forgive those who left the church and keep moving forward. I learned that those whom God had ordained to be with me would stay, and those who were never meant to be with me would eventually leave.

Psalm 30:5 (KJV) says, *"Weeping may endure for a night, but joy cometh in the morning."* Everyone's morning comes at a different time, but when you make it through midnight, you will experience the joy of a new day.

Conclusion: The Breaking of Day

As a midnight leader, you will experience pain, betrayal, and isolation. But if you can pray through it, praise through it, and lean on the power of God, you will make it through to the breaking of day. Your midnight may be dark, but it is not the end. God's mercy is new every morning, and His power will sustain you through the darkest of times.

Remember, your midnight is only temporary. Once you've endured it, you'll rise stronger and more equipped to lead through whatever challenges come your way.

Marinate for an Impact:

1. How do you typically respond to pain or betrayal in your leadership, and how can you prevent yourself from "locking up" emotionally or spiritually?

2. In what ways can you incorporate prayer and praise into your leadership during your own midnight seasons?

3. Reflect on a time when God's power sustained you through a difficult leadership challenge. How did that experience prepare you for future obstacles?

Chapter 5
Leading Beyond the Now

An impactful leader doesn't just live in the moment but looks beyond the present to shape a better future. Enjoying the present moment is important, but a visionary leader sees beyond "now" to make things even better. A prime example of this is Nick Saban, head coach of the Alabama Crimson Tide football team. Despite his team's success during a game, Saban never becomes complacent. Even when winning, he pushes his players to remain focused and disciplined because he knows that this game isn't the last one—they have more to face. Saban doesn't allow his players to develop bad habits, even in victory. His leadership philosophy is about creating long-term success, not just celebrating the moment. Saban has won an incredible 7 national championships as of 2021, further proving that his focus on excellence and looking beyond the now yields remarkable results.

Avoiding Complacency

One of the traits of a leader who leads beyond the now is avoiding complacency. It's easy to feel satisfied when things are going well, but an impactful leader asks, "What can I do to make this better?" A leader who only patches up problems without fully resolving them risks larger issues down the line. A small leak left unattended can eventually sink the entire ship. Proverbs 22:3 (KJV) says, *"A prudent man foreseeth the evil, and hideth himself: but the simple pass on, and are punished."* As leaders, we must foresee potential issues and deal with them thoroughly, not just cover them temporarily.

A leader looks for areas of improvement even when things seem good. They continue to push forward, recognizing that there's greatness in their team or organization that can still be drawn out. As Philippians 3:13-14 (KJV) reminds us, *"Brethren, I count not myself to have apprehended: but this one thing I do, forgetting those things which are behind, and reaching forth unto those things which are before, I press toward the mark for the prize of the high calling of God in Christ Jesus."* Pressing forward requires continually striving for better, not becoming satisfied with what is now.

David's Leadership Beyond the Now

A great biblical example of leading beyond the now is David during his time in the cave of Adullam. He was surrounded by men who were distressed, in debt, and discontented (1 Samuel 22:2, KJV). Though these men were broken in their current state, David looked beyond the now and trained them to become mighty men of valor. Eventually, these men became renowned for their bravery and strength (2 Samuel 23:8-39, KJV). David led them beyond their present circumstances by building them up for the future.

David's vision wasn't limited to what was happening in the cave. He saw potential in these men and invested in them for the long term. As leaders, we must see beyond our current resources and team dynamics, and work toward a greater future. Hebrews 11:1 (KJV) tells us, *"Now faith is the substance of things hoped for, the evidence of things not seen."* Leaders must have faith that their efforts now will yield results later.

Overcoming the Temptation of Settling

One of the challenges leaders face is the temptation to settle for "okay" or "good enough." However, impactful leaders are never satisfied with mediocrity. They continually ask, "How can I make this better? How can I make this greater?" This mindset requires overcoming the temptation to be content with what seems adequate. James 1:4 (KJV) encourages us to let *"patience have her perfect work, that ye may be perfect and entire, wanting nothing."* Perfection in leadership involves consistently working toward improvement and greater outcomes.

Leaders who lead beyond the now don't simply react to situations— they anticipate what's coming and prepare for it. For instance, in my own leadership journey, I've always prepared my church for the future. When I cast vision for the upcoming year, I start working with my leaders months in advance. By the time January arrives, I've already mapped out the year and am projecting towards December. Leading beyond the now means consistently preparing for what's ahead, not just focusing on the immediate.

Leading Beyond Now in Personal Leadership

In my personal life, leading beyond the now has been a guiding principle both in my family and my church. For example, with my son Jamel, I saw potential in him when he was much younger. I would get him up at five in the morning, training and investing in him. We were doing things in the now, but I was preparing him for the future. Both of my children may not have always liked the discipline and the training, but it was about laying a foundation for their success later in life. Proverbs 22:6 (KJV) says, *"Train up a child in the way he should go: and when he is old, he will not depart from it."* I was leading Jamel towards later.

With my church, the same principle applies. I don't wait until January 1st to cast vision for the new year. Instead, I start developing the vision months earlier in October. I meet with my leaders, and we work on planning for the entire year ahead. By the time the new year arrives, we're already prepared to hit the ground running. I'm always projecting forward, ensuring that we're leading beyond the now and anticipating the future.

The Danger of Failing to Lead Beyond the Now: King Saul

A biblical example of someone who failed to lead beyond the now is King Saul. Initially, Saul was a successful leader, slaying thousands of enemies (1 Samuel 18:7, KJV). But when Goliath challenged Israel, Saul faltered. He was so caught up in his past victories that he couldn't see the threat that Goliath posed to the future of Israel. Rather than taking immediate action, he hesitated and allowed fear to take over. In contrast, David saw the bigger picture. He knew that defeating Goliath wasn't just about winning the present battle—it was about securing Israel's future. David declared in 1 Samuel 17:37 (KJV), *"The Lord that delivered me out of the paw of the lion, and out of the paw of the bear, he will deliver me out of the hand of this Philistine."* David's past experiences prepared him for future victories because he always looked beyond the now.

Saul's failure to act resulted in the Philistines continuing to oppress Israel. When leaders only focus on what's in front of them, they risk missing the bigger picture and putting their people in danger. Proverbs 29:18 (KJV) says, *"Where there is no vision, the people perish."* Leaders must have a vision for the future and act decisively in the present to secure that future.

Lessons Learned from Failing to Lead Beyond the Now

When leaders fail to look beyond the now, they risk stagnation and defeat. Saul's downfall was his inability to lead beyond his immediate victories. He became complacent and lost sight of the larger mission. In contrast, David saw the future implications of every battle and led with that vision in mind.

In leadership, whether in family, ministry, or business, we must avoid the temptation to settle for the present. We must always be asking, "What can I do now that will prepare us for what's coming later?" It is this mindset that leads to lasting impact and success.

Conclusion: Always Leading Beyond the Now

Leading beyond the now requires discipline, vision, and a commitment to excellence. It involves recognizing that the actions we take today lay the foundation for tomorrow's victories. As leaders, we must avoid complacency and continuously strive to improve. We must see beyond the present challenges and work towards future success, both for ourselves and those we lead.

Marinate for an Impact:

1. How can you actively avoid complacency in your leadership, and what steps can you take to ensure continual growth and improvement for your team or organization?

2. In what areas of your leadership are you tempted to settle for "good enough," and how can you push beyond the now to prepare for future success?

3. Reflecting on David's leadership in the cave of Adullam, how can you invest in those around you now to help them grow into their potential for the future?

Chapter 6
A Well Leader

M any leaders excel in their spiritual gifts—whether as pastors, prophets, evangelists, or teachers—but truly effective leadership requires more. Leadership that extends beyond the pulpit and spiritual gifts is essential for those who want to excel in ministry and make a lasting impact. This type of leadership, referred to here as "well leadership," focuses on building influence, fostering excellence, developing teams, and ultimately leading people beyond their immediate ministry roles.

This chapter will delve into the characteristics and skills that define a well leader—someone who knows how to effectively influence people, manage resources, and carry out their vision with strategy and wisdom, much like Joseph from the Bible. While Joseph's gift of dream interpretation brought him into Pharaoh's courts, it was his ability to lead well that positioned him over all of Egypt.

Genesis 41:41-42 (KJV) reads, *"And Pharaoh said unto Joseph, See, I have set thee over all the land of Egypt. And Pharaoh took off his ring from his hand, and put it upon Joseph's hand, and arrayed him in vestures of fine linen, and put a gold chain about his neck."* Joseph's rise to power wasn't just because of his gift; it was his leadership skills that elevated him to oversee the entire land.

Winning People: Building Influence Beyond the Pulpit

A well leader understands that leadership is first and foremost about influence. As Proverbs 11:30 (KJV) says, *"The fruit of the righteous is a tree of life; and he that winneth souls is wise."* Winning people is more than just gaining followers; it is about cultivating strong relationships, earning trust, and creating a team that believes in the vision you are leading them toward.

A key to leading well is recognizing that people must be won before any task can be accomplished. A well leader influences others by building rapport, investing time into those around them, and consistently demonstrating care and concern. People respond not just to a message preached from the pulpit, but to the ways their leader engages them in everyday life. The pulpit is often seen as the culmination of leadership, but the real work of leadership is done behind the scenes.

Winning people involves working with others to carry out tasks beyond the platform of the church. Whether you are leading deacons, ushers, or ministry teams, a well leader emphasizes excellence and cultivates a spirit of unity among the team members. This process begins with winning people to your vision and creating an environment where they feel valued and empowered.

Emphasizing Excellence: A Hallmark of Leadership

Leadership is more than just getting people to follow; it's about ensuring that they are striving for excellence in everything they do. As Colossians 3:23 (KJV) says, *"And whatsoever ye do, do it heartily, as to the Lord, and not unto men."* Excellence should be the standard that well leaders set for themselves and for those they lead.

A well leader cultivates a culture of excellence by setting high expectations and leading by example. Whether it's ensuring that things are organized for a church event or creating an atmosphere of professionalism within ministry teams, a well leader knows that excellence attracts people and inspires them to do their best. Excellence is not limited to preaching or teaching—it extends to every area of leadership, from administrative tasks to interpersonal relationships.

One critical aspect of excellence is preparation. Before stepping into the pulpit, a well leader has already done the work of leading those around them, whether by organizing teams, delegating responsibilities, or simply making sure everything is in place for a successful service or event. When leaders emphasize excellence, they win people over and create an atmosphere where everyone is inspired to give their best.

Fostering a Culture of Learning

A well leader is also a learner, constantly seeking to grow and improve in their role. Proverbs 1:5 (KJV) reminds us, *"A wise man will hear, and will increase learning; and a man of understanding shall attain unto wise counsels."* Part of leading well is fostering a culture where learning is valued, both for the leader and for the team.

Leadership requires a constant posture of learning—learning from mistakes, learning from successes, and always seeking ways to improve the team's performance. Well leaders are not only learners themselves but also encourage those around them to grow. By doing so, they create a dynamic where everyone on the team is invested in becoming better, leading to a more effective and productive ministry.

To lead well, one must lean on others, collaborate, and draw strength from the gifts and talents of the people around them. Just as Proverbs 27:17 (KJV) states, *"Iron sharpeneth iron; so a man sharpeneth the countenance of his friend."* A well leader understands that learning and growth come through collaboration and the willingness to listen to the ideas and input of others.

Strategizing for Success: The Importance of Planning and Execution

Leadership is not just about casting vision; it's also about executing that vision with precision and care. Proverbs 21:5 (KJV) says, *"The thoughts of the diligent tend only to plenteousness; but of every one that is hasty only to want."* A well leader knows that success requires strategy and that every plan must be carefully thought out and executed.

Joseph's story demonstrates the importance of strategy in leadership. As he prepared Egypt for the coming famine, he developed a plan, gathered resources, and implemented a system that would sustain the nation through seven years of scarcity. His ability to lead well was evident not just in his spiritual gifts but in his strategic thinking and ability to manage people and resources effectively.

In ministry, leading well means being a strategist—knowing how to plan, how to delegate, and how to execute your vision. Whether it's organizing a church event, building a team, or preparing for a large-scale outreach, a well leader understands the importance of having a strategy in place. They don't just react to situations; they proactively plan for success.

The Work of Leadership: Building and Leading Teams

Leadership is a team effort. A well leader knows that they cannot accomplish their vision alone—they need a team to support them and help carry out the work. Ecclesiastes 4:9 (KJV) reminds us, *"Two are better than one; because they have a good reward for their labour."* A well leader knows how to build, recruit, train, and oversee a team that shares the vision and works together to accomplish the goals of the ministry.

One of the greatest examples of team building is Nehemiah, who led the people of Israel in rebuilding the walls of Jerusalem. Nehemiah 4:6 (KJV) says, *"So built we the wall; and all the wall was joined together unto the half thereof: for the people had a mind to work."* Nehemiah's success was not just in his vision but in his ability to lead the people in a unified effort to accomplish a great task.

A well leader knows that their success is directly tied to the success of their team. By building a strong team, delegating responsibilities, and creating an environment where everyone is working toward a common goal, a well leader is able to accomplish much more than they could on their own.

Conclusion: Becoming a Well Leader

A well leader is someone who goes beyond their ministry gift to lead with wisdom, strategy, and care. They know how to win people, cultivate excellence, foster learning, strategize for success, and build strong teams. By doing so, they are able to lead not only within the church but also in the broader community, making a lasting impact on those they serve.

Leadership is not just about what happens in the pulpit; it's about what happens in the everyday interactions, the planning, the strategizing, and the building of relationships. By becoming a well leader, you will be able to influence and impact people in ways that go far beyond your spiritual gifts, leading them toward the vision and purpose that God has placed on your life.

Marinate for an Impact:

1. In what ways can you cultivate excellence in your leadership, both in your spiritual gift and in your daily interactions with those you lead?

2. How can you foster a culture of learning within your team or ministry, ensuring that everyone is growing and improving together?

3. Reflecting on Joseph's ability to lead with strategy and wisdom, how can you better plan and execute your vision to ensure long-term success for your ministry or organization?

Chapter 7
The Leader of Leaders

L et's talk about a leader's leader—someone who leads not just followers but also other leaders. The question becomes, what's the benefit or blessing of learning to lead leaders?

One of the first blessings or benefits of leading leaders is that your influence is multiplied. When you are only leading followers, it limits your influence because it normally stops with the followers, as they are not leaders themselves. But when you learn how to lead leaders, it increases your influence and multiplies it because those leaders, in turn, lead their own followers. This creates a ripple effect where your influence extends far beyond your immediate circle. Proverbs 11:14 (KJV) reminds us, *"Where no counsel is, the people fall: but in the multitude of counsellors there is safety."* Leading leaders ensures that there is a multitude of wise counsel, expanding the reach and impact of your leadership.

Another benefit is that you have a lasting impact. Leading leaders helps build a legacy, as you are not just influencing followers but also mentoring and shaping other leaders who will continue to lead even after you are gone. This ensures that the principles and values you instill will endure. The Apostle Paul exemplified this in his relationship with Timothy, as he instructed him in 2 Timothy 2:2 (KJV): *"And the things that thou hast heard of me among many witnesses, the same commit thou to faithful men, who shall be able to teach others also."*

The Power of Influence

A leader of leaders holds a position of significant influence, not just over their own followers, but over other leaders. This influence allows you to guide, mentor, and shape them into effective leaders. You become a model of what true leadership looks like. This is why it is so important to learn how to lead leaders. You are shaping the future of leadership itself. Jesus exemplified this as He mentored His disciples, especially Peter, James, and John, who would go on to lead others. In Matthew 16:18-19 (KJV), Jesus says to Peter, *"And I say also unto thee, That thou art Peter, and upon this rock I will build my church; and the gates of hell shall not prevail against it. And I will give unto thee the keys of the kingdom of heaven..."* Jesus, as the leader of leaders, imparted authority and responsibility to Peter, empowering him to continue His mission.

The Difference Between a Leader and *The* Leader

It's essential to understand the difference between *a* leader and *the* leader. A leader is someone who has influence, respect, and authority in a certain capacity, but *the* leader is someone who leads leaders. The leader is the one at the top, where the "buck stops." A leader may manage followers, but *the* leader manages and leads other leaders. This position requires a higher level of responsibility, vision, and strategic thinking. As the leader, you are responsible for the development of other leaders.

When Paul spoke of his leadership, he understood this role. In Acts 20:28 (KJV), Paul charged the elders of the church with these words: *"Take heed therefore unto yourselves, and to all the flock, over the which the Holy Ghost hath made you overseers, to feed the church of God, which he hath purchased with his own blood."* Paul was not just speaking to followers; he was speaking to other leaders and urging them to be vigilant in their leadership.

The Dangers of Not Knowing How to Lead Leaders

Failing to learn how to lead leaders can cause several dangers:

1. **Loss of Influence:** If you do not understand the dynamics of leading leaders, you may lose influence over them. They may not respect you as much because they expect more from their leader than followers do. Leading leaders requires a deeper understanding of how to challenge and motivate them.

2. **Undeveloped Leaders:** If you do not develop the leaders under you, they may become stagnant and ultimately walk away. It is essential to shape and mold them for greater capacity and potential. Proverbs 27:17 (KJV) says, *"Iron sharpeneth iron; so a man sharpeneth the countenance of his friend."* You must be the one who sharpens and refines these leaders, helping them reach their full potential.

3. **Resistance from Leaders:** If leaders feel that they are being treated like followers instead of leaders, they may begin to resist your direction. This resistance can lead to a loss of credibility and value in their eyes. Leaders respond differently than followers because they are accustomed to leading themselves. You must

know how to guide strong-willed leaders without undermining their leadership.

4. **Stifling Growth:** Another danger is stifling the growth of your organization or ministry because you cannot handle the strong personalities and capabilities of other leaders. A leader must learn how to navigate the challenges of leading leaders to prevent the organization from stalling.

Paul: A Leader of Leaders

Paul was an exemplary leader of leaders. He had what every leader of leaders needs: the ability to be led, to lead others, and to develop future leaders.

-   **Paul Was Led:** Paul was led by great mentors and teachers, such as Gamaliel, as seen in Acts 22:3 (KJV): *"I am verily a man which am a Jew, born in Tarsus, a city in Cilicia, yet brought up in this city at the feet of Gamaliel, and taught according to the perfect manner of the law of the fathers, and was zealous toward God, as ye all are this day."* Paul had leaders who poured into him and prepared him for his role as a leader of leaders.

-   **Paul Led Others:** Paul did not just receive leadership; he passed it on. One of his key mentees was Timothy, to whom he imparted leadership and wisdom. In 1 Timothy 1:2 (KJV), Paul refers to Timothy as *"my own son in the faith,"* demonstrating the deep relationship and influence he had over Timothy as a leader of leaders.

-   **Paul Developed Leaders:** Paul not only led Timothy but equipped him to lead others, thus ensuring the continuity of leadership. His ability to lead leaders was essential to the spread of the gospel and the growth of the early church. Paul's influence extended beyond his own generation because he understood how to build and develop future leaders.

The Importance of Learning to Lead Leaders

It is crucial for every leader to develop the ability to lead other leaders. The role comes with greater responsibility and requires a higher level of wisdom, patience, and strategic thinking. Leading leaders is not just about managing; it is about empowering and multiplying your influence for lasting impact. Paul exemplified this, as did Jesus. Jesus led leaders like Peter, who went on to build the church, and Paul, who carried the gospel to the Gentiles.

As a leader of leaders, you must be able to:

- **Multiply Influence:** Your leadership doesn't end with the people you directly lead; it extends through the leaders you develop. This increases your impact exponentially.

- **Create Lasting Impact:** By developing leaders, you are building a legacy that will outlast your own tenure. Just as Paul's work continues through the church today, your influence will extend into the future through the leaders you have mentored.

- **Adapt to Stronger Personalities:** Leading leaders requires a different approach than leading followers. You must adapt to the personalities, capacities, and experiences of those who are used to leading others.

Conclusion: Leading Leaders to Lead

Leading leaders is a unique and powerful form of leadership. It requires a deep understanding of influence, respect, and development. Just as Paul led Timothy, and Jesus led Peter, we too must rise to the challenge of leading leaders. It's not enough to lead followers; the true mark of a great leader is the ability to raise up other leaders. Let us strive to be leaders of leaders, creating a lasting legacy and multiplying our influence for the Kingdom of God.

Marinate for an Impact:

1. How can you multiply your influence by intentionally developing the leaders under your care to lead others effectively?

2. In what ways can you adapt your leadership approach to meet the needs of strong-willed leaders while maintaining your influence and credibility?

3. Reflecting on Paul's example, how can you ensure that the leaders you mentor will continue to carry forward the vision and legacy you've established?

Conclusion

Thank you for joining me on this journey of discovering what it truly means to be a leader. Throughout these pages, we've explored the various facets of leadership, delving deep into what it takes to lead with purpose, strength, and integrity. I pray that the lessons shared here have encouraged and inspired you to grow in your own leadership, understanding that leadership is never about elevating ourselves but always about serving Him—Jesus Christ.

In all that we have learned, let us never forget that Jesus is the ultimate example of leadership. He exemplifies every trait of a great leader, and it is His life and actions that we must seek to emulate in our own leadership journey.

Jesus is, first and foremost, the **Servant Leader**. In John 13:14-15 (KJV), He demonstrated this by washing the feet of His disciples, taking up a towel and humbling Himself to serve them. True leadership is rooted in humility, not in the title we carry but the towel we have to serve others.

Jesus is also the **Focused Leader**. Luke 9:51 (KJV) says, *"And it came to pass, when the time was come that he should be received up, he stedfastly set his face to go to Jerusalem."* He was fully committed to His mission, setting His face toward Jerusalem, knowing that suffering awaited Him. Yet, He remained unwavering in His focus, determined to fulfill the Father's will, no matter the cost.

Not only was Jesus the Servant Leader and Focused Leader, but He was also a **Trained Leader**. In Luke 2:46-47 (KJV), we find Jesus as a young boy, sitting in the temple, astonishing the teachers with His understanding and answers. From an early age, He was filled with wisdom and knowledge, prepared and trained for the mission ahead.

Jesus was also the **Midnight Leader**, leading through the darkest times. In Matthew 26:38-39 (KJV), He prayed in the Garden of Gethsemane, *"My soul is exceeding sorrowful, even unto death: tarry ye here, and watch with me."* Even in His agony, Jesus faithfully led by example, submitting to the Father's will and showing us how to navigate the darkest hours with faith and prayer.

Moreover, Jesus is the **Leader Beyond the Now**. In John 16:13 (KJV), He prepared His followers for the coming of the Holy Spirit, saying, *"Howbeit when he, the Spirit of truth, is come, he will guide you into all truth... and he will shew you things to come."* Jesus always looked beyond the present moment, preparing His followers for what was to come and equipping them for long-term success.

Jesus also exemplified the **Well Leader**. In John 10:11 (KJV), He said, *"I am the good shepherd: the good shepherd giveth his life for the sheep."* As the Good Shepherd, Jesus led with compassion, protection, and sacrifice. He cared for His followers deeply, even to the point of laying down His life for them.

Conclusion

Finally, Jesus is the **Leader of Leaders**. In Matthew 28:18-20 (KJV), Jesus commissioned His disciples to go and make disciples of all nations, saying, *"All power is given unto me in heaven and in earth. Go ye therefore, and teach all nations, baptizing them in the name of the Father, and of the Son, and of the Holy Ghost: Teaching them to observe all things whatsoever I have commanded you: and, lo, I am with you alway, even unto the end of the world."* Jesus empowered His disciples to become leaders, spreading His message and raising up future leaders. He is the ultimate Leader of Leaders, showing us how to lead with authority, guidance, and purpose.

As you move forward in your leadership journey, always remember that Jesus is our perfect example. He showed us how to serve with humility, lead with focus, train for our mission, persevere through difficulties, prepare for the future, care for others, and empower the next generation of leaders. Let His life be your model, and let His Spirit guide you in all that you do. For in Him, we find the fullness of what it truly means to be a leader.

About The Author

Dr.Clinton P Cornelius has served as the Senior Pastor of Peaceful Believer's Church in Fort Meade, FL for 29 years. Pastor Cornelius is a man called by God to serve this generation and confront them with the cause of Christ. Saved and filled with the Holy Spirit while in high school, he is a dynamic preacher and teacher who is enthusiastic about sharing the word of God. One of his greatest joys as Pastor is watching the people of God grow as they apply the principles of God's word to their lives daily. Under the headship of God, Pastor Cornelius has provided strong, effective leadership to the PBC congregation, enabling them to develop and mature as saints.

His life and ministry are submitted and accountable first to God, then to the leadership of Covenant Connections International founded by the late Apostle Bishop Nathaniel Holcomb of the Christian House of Prayer Ministries in Killeen, TX, where Overseer Valerie Holcomb is presently Pastor.

Dr. Cornelius holds a Bachelor of Arts in Theology, a Masters, and a Doctoral Degree in Theology from Minnesota Graduate School of Theology. He is married to the former Frenchie Jackson of Fort Meade, FL, who serves with him at PBC. They have two adult children, Jemalle and Ashli, and eight grandchildren.

Pastor C is the Founder and President of CPC Ministries and Impact Development of Central Florida, a nonprofit organization designed to enhance the community of Ft. Meade and its surrounding areas. He serves on several boards and committees in his city and county.

His favorite scripture is Romans 10:17: "So then faith cometh by hearing and hearing by the word of God."

Made in the USA
Columbia, SC
05 November 2024

45429277R00039